Latin:
Lumen Ad Viam.

To
Light,
is our
dedication:
three lit candles,
three Books of L,

Credit goes to
the team of designers,
photographers, cartoonists,
and editor Dr. Common Sense
at the publisher: D'Moon

Copyright ©D'Moon
second edition, first hardcover print: 2021
ebook edition: 2014
all rights reserved except for quotes, mottos and poems

ISBN: 978-1-933187-94-5

Slight variations may occur
as part of the print-on-demand process
since each book is manufactured in its entirety.

Your feedback is most welcome ~
publisher@worldculturepictorial.com

BOOK OF L²

Quotable Wit & Wisdom

Dr. Common Sense
dimom books

Publisher's Note

Legacy of the old Latin Fiat Lux
"Let there be Light", like lightning,
inspiring minds from ancient Rome
to digital age, lighting up lakes,
leaves, illuminating hues of
landscape, at this very moment
sheds light onto this Book of L.

"L", a magic ring, holds key words about
Life which is like a line, drawn by
looking deep, listening and learning, by
laboring brain and limbs, and by
leisure; dotted by being lost to fame or
luxury, lured by lust,
laden with desire for lots of lots. Or,
Life can also simply tune in to
lovely music, light footsteps and
laughter, cheery or without choice.

Book of L sees
L in Quotation,
L in Latin Motto, and
L in Poem. Poetry lives beyond
literature, and poets are beyond masters of
languages. Their passion and expression,
brilliance and down-to-earth
cutting wit spark lightning,
lighting up centuries' space time and the way
for generations after generations! Reading
lines from classic poems, heritage to all, is
indeed amusing.

Latin: "Lumen Ad Viam".
Buddha: "Thousands of candles can be
lit from a single candle, and the
life of the candle will not be shortened.
Happiness never decreases by being shared."

Therefore, to Light, is our dedication
~ three lit candles, three Books of L.
Enjoy, dear readers.

Dr. Common Sense

Contents

Dedication
Copyright
Title Page
Publisher's Note
Table of Contents

Section 1 : L in Quotation

Love
- love you more
Lady
- Lady Nancy Astor
Laurel
- win the laurel
Light
- landscapes, variety from light
Lend
- lend money if you don't need it

Book of L² - Quotable Wit and Wisdom
Contents

Listen
- sit down and listen
Love
- the love that lasts the longest
Life
- life affords no higher...
Live
- do not neglect to live
Life
- quality of life
Life
- to the edge, then a leap taken
Letter
- literal translations? the letter kills
Leader
- leader, learn more
Live
- utter words? or to live by them

Dr. Common Sense
Contents

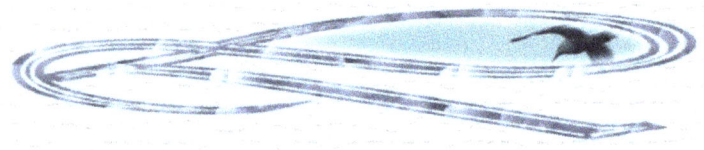

Lost
- lost to fame

Luck
- good luck

Logic
- logic vs. imagination

Laughter
- day without laughter

Laughable
- more laughable

Look
- dressed in overalls: looks like work

Liberty
- be a king vs. forfeit liberty

Long
- takes a long time

Lengthen
- mirth and merriment lengthens life

Book of L² - Quotable Wit and Wisdom

Contents

Loyal
- one loyal friend vs. ten thousand relatives

Line
- yes, no, a straight line, a goal

Like
- like an ancient philosopher

Little
- use brain too little:
lazy habits of thinking

Little
- pitied a little,
praised a little,
appreciated a little

Little
- dare a little more

Language
- language the deaf can hear

Dr. Common Sense

Contents

Lecture
- lecture rooms vs.
genuinely thirst after truth and justice

Lesson
- lessons lived

Leopard
- leopard's credit

Leaf
- trembling of a leaf

Last
- comedian can only last 'til

Lie
- lie close, like light and shadow

Latitude
- latitude allowed

Lay
- hours laid out

Book of L² - Quotable Wit and Wisdom
Contents

Lend
- neighbors gladly lend and borrow
Lip
- not my lips you kissed
Land
- the Land and its People
Learn
- likewise should learn to hear it

Section 2 : L in Latin Motto

Labore
- Labore et Honore
Lex
- Lux et Lex
Lumine
- In Lumine Sapientia

Dr. Common Sense
Contents

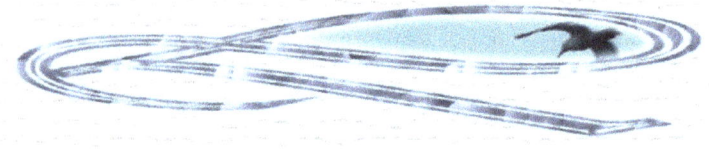

Lux
- Lux et Veritas
Lux
- Fiat Lux
Luce
- Crescente Luce
Lumen
- In Lumine Tuo Videmus Lumen
Longa
- Ars Longa, Vita Brevis
Lux
- Lux sit
Liberabit
- Veritas vos Liberabit
Lux
- Lux

Book of L ^{2} - Quotable Wit and Wisdom

Contents

Libertas
- Libertas Perfundet Omnia Luce

Lux
- Lux in Domino

Lucem
- Lucem Sequimur

Libertas
- Veritas - Iustitia - Libertas

Lux
- Lux Hominum Vita

Lux
- Post Nubes, Lux

Luceat
- Luceat Lux Vestra

Dr. Common Sense
Contents

Section 3 : L in Poem

Lear, Lute, Let

Sonnet. Written Before Re-Read King Lear
by John Keats
"O golden-tongued Romance with serene lute!
Shut up thine olden pages, and be mute:
Begetters of our deep eternal theme,
Let me not wander in a barren dream"

Lines, Length, Long, Life, Little, Love, Less

Lines Composed
A Few Miles Above Tintern Abbey
by William Wordsworth
"Five years, five summers, with length
Of five long winters!
On that best portion of a good man's life,
His little, nameless, unremembered, acts
Of kindness and of love. Nor less"

Book of L² - Quotable Wit and Wisdom

Contents

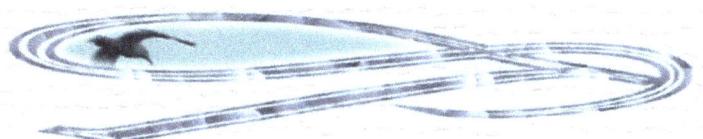

Lord, Library, Lawless

On the Same -
(On the Burning of Lord Mansfield's Library)
by William Cowper
"When wit and genius meet their doom,
They tell us of the fate of Rome,
The lawless herd, with fury blind,
The flowers are gone, - but still we find..."

Luminous, Long, Little

Winter-Solitude
by Archibald Lampman
"on a luminous pale-gray sky;
a long thin cloud above the colour of August rye.
Where the thin wind stung my cheeks,
and the hard snow ran in little ripples and peaks"

Dr. Common Sense
Contents

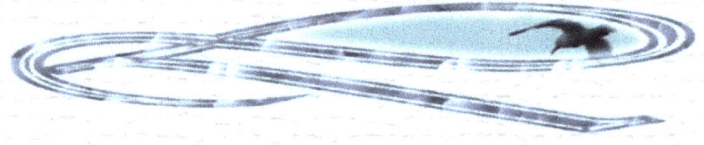

Leaves, Late, Life, Lichens

Leaves Compared with Flowers
by Robert Frost
"A tree's leaves may be ever so good,
So may its bar, so may its wood;
Late in life I have come on fern.
Now lichens are due to have their turn"

Laugh, Lively

Laughing Song
by William Blake
"When the green woods laugh with the voice of joy,
And the dimpling stream runs laughing by;
when the meadows laugh with lively green,
And the grasshopper laughs in the merry scene"

Book of L² - Quotable Wit and Wisdom

Contents

Lake, Leman, Lovely, Lore

Sonnet to Lake Leman
by Lord Byron
"Leman! Thy banks were lovely as to all,
But they have made them lovelier, for the lore
Of mighty minds doth hallow in the core"

Legacy, Leave, Less, Love, Live

A Legacy
by John Greenleaf Whittier
"I leave with thee a sense
Of hands upheld and trials rendered less,
That love, which fails of perfect utterance here,
Lives on to fill the heavenly atmosphere"

Dr. Common Sense
Contents

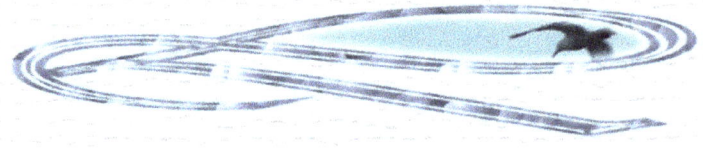

Lie

Sonnet 138
by William Shakespeare
"Therefore I lie with her, and she with me,
And in our faults by lies we flattered be"

❄❄❄

WcP Blog | World Culture Pictorial®
Other Books of L

Dr. Common Sense

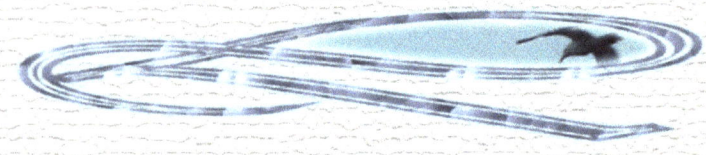

~ *Love you more* ~

"Always set high value
on spontaneous kindness.
He whose inclination
prompts him to cultivate
your friendship of his own accord
will love you more than one whom
you have been at pains to attach to you."
- Samuel Johnson

Book of L ² - Quotable Wit and Wisdom

~ Lady Nancy Astor ~

"Lady Nancy Astor:
'Winston, if you were my husband,
I'd poison your tea.'

Churchill:
'Nancy, if I were your husband,
I'd drink it.' "
- Winston Churchill

Dr. Common Sense

~ win the Laurel ~

"Force may subdue,
but love gains,
and he that forgives first
wins the laurel."
- William Penn

Book of L ² - Quotable Wit and Wisdom

~ *Landscapes,
variety from Light* ~

"All of our actions take their hue
from the complexion of the heart,
as landscapes their variety from light."
- Francis Bacon

Dr. Common Sense

~ *Lend money
if you don't need it* ~

"A bank is a place
that will lend you money
if you can prove that you don't need it."
- Bob Hope

Book of L ² - Quotable Wit and Wisdom

~ *sit down and* ℒ*isten* ~

"Courage is what it takes
to stand up and speak;
courage is also what it takes
to sit down and listen."
- Winston Churchill

Dr. Common Sense

~ the Love that Lasts the Longest ~

"The love that lasts the longest
is the love that is never returned."
- William Somerset Maugham

Book of L² - Quotable Wit and Wisdom

~ *Life affords no higher...* ~

"Life affords no higher pleasure
than that of surmounting difficulties,
passing from one step of success
to another, forming new wishes
and seeing them gratified."
- Samuel Johnson

Dr. Common Sense

~ *do not neglect to Live* ~

"When making your choice in life,
do not neglect to live."
- Samuel Johnson

Book of L² - Quotable Wit and Wisdom

~ quality of Life ~

"For quality of life"
- motto, Wageningen University

Dr. Common Sense

~ to the edge,
then a Leap taken ~

"Life is traveling
to the edge of knowledge,
then a leap taken."
- D. H. Lawrence

~ Literal translations? the Letter kills ~

"Woe to the makers of literal translations,
who by rendering every word
weaken the meaning!
It is indeed by so doing that we can say
the letter kills
and the spirit gives life."
- Voltaire

Dr. Common Sense

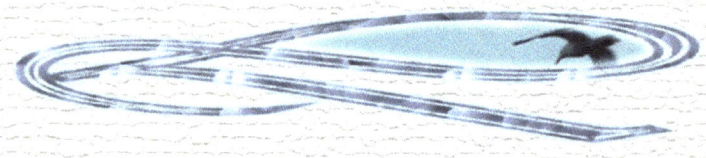

~ *Leader, Learn more* ~

"If your actions inspire others
to dream more, learn more,
do more and become more,
you are a leader."
- John Quincy Adams

Book of L ² - Quotable Wit and Wisdom

~ after words?
or to Live by them ~

"As we express our gratitude,
we must never forget
that the highest appreciation
is not to utter words,
but to live by them."
- John F. Kennedy

Dr. Common Sense

~ *Lost to fame* ~

"May the countryside
and the gliding valley streams
content me.
Lost to fame,
let me love river and woodland."
- Virgil Publius Vergilius Maro

Book of L ^{2} - Quotable Wit and Wisdom

~ good Luck ~

"Good night,
and good luck."
- Edward R. Murrow

Dr. Common Sense

~ Logic vs. imagination ~

"Logic will get you from A to B.
Imagination will take you everywhere."
- Albert Einstein

Book of L² - Quotable Wit and Wisdom

~ day without Laughter ~

"The most wasted of all days
is one without Laughter."
- E. E. Cummings

Dr. Common Sense

~ more Laughable ~

"I know of nothing more laughable
than a doctor who does not die of old age."
- Voltaire

Book of L ² - Quotable Wit and Wisdom

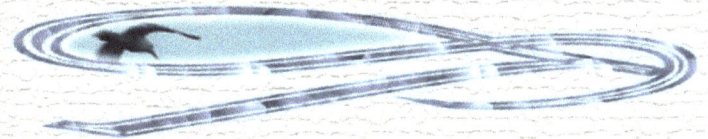

dressed in overalls:
Looks Like work ~

"Opportunity is missed by most people
because it is dressed in overalls
and looks like work."
- Thomas A. Edison

Dr. Common Sense

~ *be a king vs. forfeit Liberty* ~

"I would rather not be a king
than to forfeit my liberty."
- Phaedrus

Book of L ² - Quotable Wit and Wisdom

~ takes a *Long* time ~

"It takes a long time
to become young."
- Pablo Picasso

Dr. Common Sense

~ mirth and merriment Lengthens Life ~

"Frame thy mind
to mirth and merriment,
which bars a thousand harms,
and lengthens life."
- William Shakespeare

Book of L ² - Quotable Wit and Wisdom

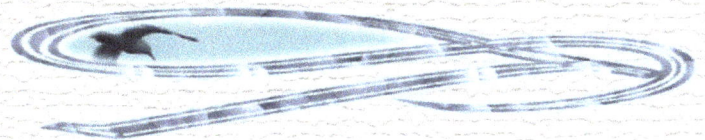

~ one Loyal friend vs. ten thousand relatives ~

"One loyal friend
is worth ten thousand relatives."
- Euripides

Dr. Common Sense

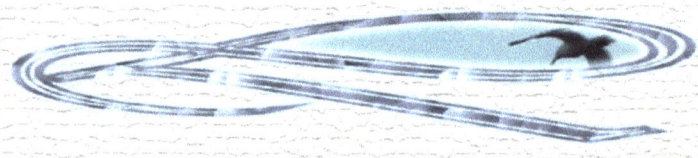

~ yes, no, a straight Line, a goal ~

"The formula for my happiness:
a Yes, a No,
a straight line, a goal."
- Friedrich Nietzsche

Book of L ² - Quotable Wit and Wisdom

~ *Like*
an ancient philosopher ~

"Christmas was close at hand,
in all his bluff and hearty honesty;
it was the season of hospitality,
merriment, and open-heartedness;
the old year was preparing,
like an ancient philosopher,
to call his friends around him,
and amidst the sound of feasting and revelry
to pass gently and calmly away."
- Charles Dickens

Dr. Common Sense

use brain too Little: Lazy habits of thinking ~

"Reading, after a certain age, diverts the mind too much from its creative pursuits. Any man who reads too much and uses his own brain too little falls into lazy habits of thinking."
- Albert Einstein

Book of L ² - Quotable Wit and Wisdom

*~ pitied a Little,
praised a Little,
appreciated a Little ~*

"All that a husband or wife really wants
is to be pitied a little,
praised a little,
and appreciated a little."
- Oliver Goldsmith

Dr. Common Sense

~ dare a Little more ~

"I speak the truth
not so much as I would,
but as much as I dare,
and I dare a little more
as I grow older."
- Michel de Montaigne

~ Language the deaf can hear ~

"Kindness is the language
which the deaf can hear
and the blind can see."
- Mark Twain

Dr. Common Sense

~ Lecture rooms vs. genuinely thirst after truth and justice ~

"Academic chairs are many,
but wise and noble teachers are few;
lecture-rooms are numerous and large,
but the number of young people
who genuinely thirst
after truth and justice
is small."
- Albert Einstein

Book of L² - Quotable Wit and Wisdom

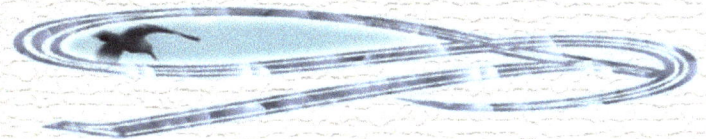

~ *Lessons Lived* ~

"Life is a succession of lessons
which must be lived
to be understood."
- Helen Keller

Dr. Common Sense

~ *Leopard's credit* ~

"A leopard does not change his spots,
or change his feeling
that spots are rather a credit."
- Ivy Compton-Burnett

Book of L ² - Quotable Wit and Wisdom

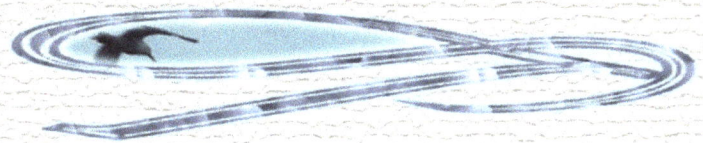

~ *trembling of a Leaf* ~

"Never say there is nothing beautiful
in the world anymore.
There is always something
to make you wonder
in the shape of a tree,
the trembling of a leaf."
- Albert Schweitzer

Dr. Common Sense

~ comedian can only
Last 'til ~

"A comedian can only last
'til he either takes himself serious
or his audience takes him serious."
- Will Rogers

Lie close, Like Light and shadow ~

"The comic and the tragic
lie inseparably close,
like light and shadow."
- Socrates

Dr. Common Sense

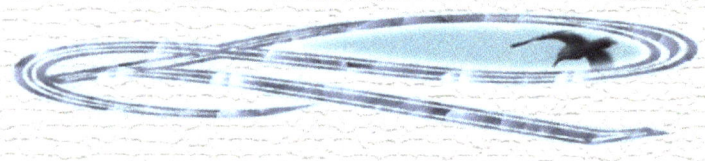

~ *Latitude allowed* ~

"The teller of a mirthful tale
has latitude allowed him.
We are content
with less than absolute truth."
- Charles Lamb

Book of L ² - Quotable Wit and Wisdom

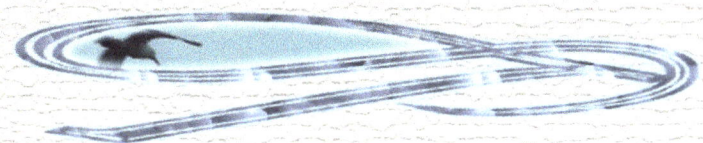

~ *hours Laid out* ~

"Gold that buys health
can never be ill spent;
nor hours laid out
in harmless merriment."
- John Webster

Dr. Common Sense

neighbors gladly Lend and borrow ~

"To God be humble,
to thy friend be kind,
and with thy neighbors
gladly lend and borrow;
His chance tonight,
it maybe thine tomorrow."
- William Dunbar

Book of L² - Quotable Wit and Wisdom

~ not my Lips you kissed ~

"For it was not into my ear
you whispered,
but into my heart.
It was not my lips
you kissed,
but my soul."
- Judy Garland

Dr. Common Sense

~ *the Land
and its People* ~

"For the Land and its People"
- motto, North Dakota State University

Book of L ² - Quotable Wit and Wisdom

Likewise should Learn to hear it ~

"In order that all men may be taught
to speak the truth,
it is necessary that all likewise
should learn to hear it."
- Samuel Johnson

Dr. Common Sense

~ *Labore* ~

"*Labore* et Honore"
"By labor and honor"
- motto,
Wyggeston and Queen Elizabeth I College

Book of L² - Quotable Wit and Wisdom

~ *Lex* ~

"*Lux* et Lex"
"Light and Law"
- motto, Franklin & Marshall College

Dr. Common Sense

~ *Lumine* ~

"*In Lumine Sapientia*"
"*In sunlight, wisdom*"
- motto, University of Almeria

Book of L² - Quotable Wit and Wisdom

~ *Lux* ~

"*Lux* et Veritas"
"Light and Truth"
- motto, Chowan University

Dr. Common Sense

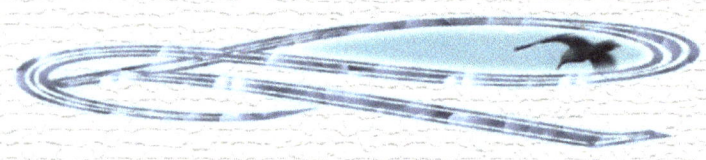

~ *Lux* ~

"*Fiat Lux*"
"*Let there be light*"
- motto, Rollins College

Book of L² - Quotable Wit and Wisdom

~ *Luce* ~

"Crescente Luce"
"Light ever increasing"
- motto, James Cook University

Dr. Common Sense

~ *Lumen* ~

"*In Lumine Tuo Videmus Lumen*"
"In Your Light we see the light"
- motto, Kampen Theological University

Book of L ² - Quotable Wit and Wisdom

~ *Longa* ~

"Ars Longa, Vita Brevis"
"Art is long, Life is short"
- motto, Silpakorn University

Dr. Common Sense

~ *Lux* ~

"*Lux* sit"
"Let there be light"
- motto, University of Washington

Book of L ² - Quotable Wit and Wisdom

~ *Liberabit* ~

"Veritas vos Liberabit"
"The Truth will set you free"
- motto, Johns Hopkins University

Dr. Common Sense

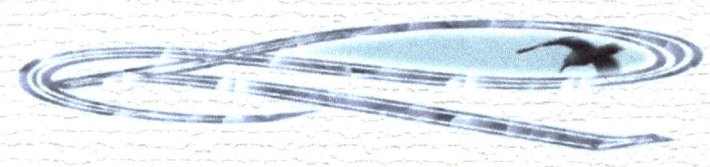

~ *Lux* ~

"*Lux*"
"Light"
- motto, Morehead State University

Book of L ² - Quotable Wit and Wisdom

~ *Libertas* ~

"Libertas Perfundet Omnia Luce"
"Liberty will flood all things with light"
- motto,
Complutense University of Madrid

Dr. Common Sense

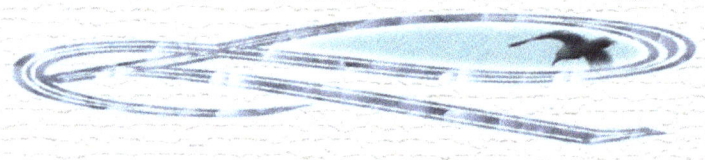

~ *Lux* ~

"*Lux* in Domino"
"Light in the Lord"
- motto, Ateneo de Manila University

Book of L ² - Quotable Wit and Wisdom

~ *Lucem* ~

"*Lucem Sequimur*"
"We follow the light"
- motto, University of Exeter

Dr. Common Sense

~ *Libertas* ~

"Veritas - Iustitia - Libertas"
"Truth - Justice - Liberty"
- motto, Free University of Berlin

Book of L² - Quotable Wit and Wisdom

~ *Lux* ~

"*Lux* Hominum Vita"

"Light the life of man"
- motto, University of New Mexico

Dr. Common Sense

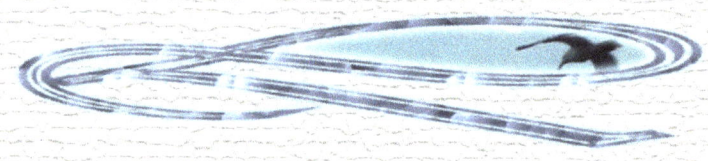

~ *Lux* ~

"Post Nubes, Lux"
"Out of darkness, light"
- motto, Cranfield University

Book of L² - Quotable Wit and Wisdom

~ *Luceat* ~

"*Luceat Lux Vestra*"
"Let your light shine"
- motto, St Patrick's College, Strathfield

Dr. Common Sense

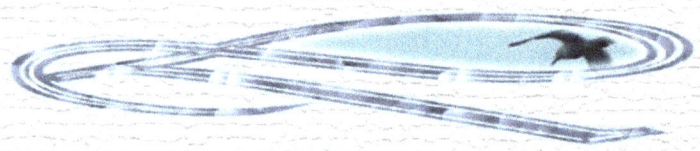

O golden-tongued Romance with serene lute!
Shut up thine olden pages, and be mute:
Begetters of our deep eternal theme,
Let me not wander in a barren dream

Sonnet.
Written Before
Re-Read King Lear
John Keats

O golden-tongued Romance with serene lute!
Fair plumed Syren! Queen of far away!
Leave melodizing on this wintry day,
Shut up thine olden pages, and be mute:
Adieu! for once again the fierce dispute,
Betwixt damnation and impassion'd clay
Must I burn through; once more humbly assay
The bitter-sweet of this Shakespearian fruit.

Book of L² - Quotable Wit and Wisdom

Chief Poet! and ye clouds of Albion,
Begetters of our deep eternal theme,
When through the old oak forest I am gone,
Let me not wander in a barren dream,
But when I am consumed in the fire,
Give me new Phoenix wings
 to fly at my desire.

Dr. Common Sense

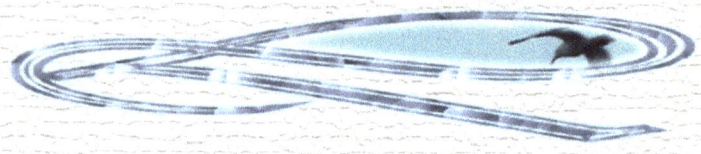

Five years, five summers, with length
Of five long winters!
On that best portion of a good man's life,
His little, nameless, unremembered, acts
Of kindness and of love. Nor less

Lines Composed
A Few Miles Above
Tintern Abbey
William Wordsworth

Five years have past;

   five summers, with the length
Of five long winters! and again I hear
These waters,
   rolling from their mountain-springs
With a soft inland murmur.--Once again
Do I behold these steep and lofty cliffs,

Book of L ² - Quotable Wit and Wisdom

That on a wild secluded scene impress
Thoughts of more deep seclusion; and connect
The landscape with the quiet of the sky.
The day is come when I again repose
Here, under this dark sycamore, and view
These plots of cottage-ground,
    these orchard-tufts,
Which at this season, with their unripe fruits,
Are clad in one green hue, and lose themselves
'Mid groves and copses. Once again I see
These hedge-rows, hardly hedge-rows,
    little lines
Of sportive wood run wild:
    these pastoral farms,
Green to the very door; and wreaths of smoke
Sent up, in silence, from among the trees!

Dr. Common Sense

With some uncertain notice, as might seem
Of vagrant dwellers in the houseless woods,
Or of some Hermit's cave, where by his fire
The Hermit sits alone.
These beauteous forms,
Through a long absence, have not been to me
As is a landscape to a blind man's eye:
But oft, in lonely rooms, and 'mid the din
Of towns and cities, I have owed to them
In hours of weariness, sensations sweet,
Felt in the blood, and felt along the heart;
And passing even into my purer mind,
With tranquil restoration:--feelings too
Of unremembered pleasure: such, perhaps,
As have no slight or trivial influence
On that best portion of a good man's life,
His little, nameless, unremembered, acts
Of kindness and of love. Nor less, I trust,

Book of L² - Quotable Wit and Wisdom

To them I may have owed another gift,
Of aspect more sublime; that blessed mood,
In which the burthen of the mystery,
In which the heavy and the weary weight
Of all this unintelligible world,
Is lightened:--that serene and blessed mood,
In which the affections gently lead us on,--
Until, the breath of this corporeal frame
And even the motion of our human blood
Almost suspended, we are laid asleep
In body, and become a living soul:
While with an eye made quiet by the power
Of harmony, and the deep power of joy,
We see into the life of things.

Dr. Common Sense

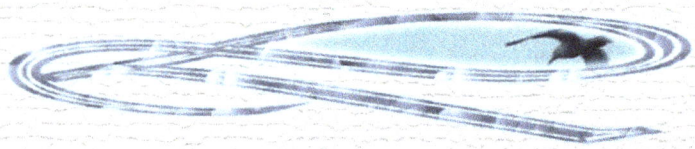

If this
Be but a vain belief, yet, oh! how oft--
In darkness and amid the many shapes
Of joyless daylight; when the fretful stir
Unprofitable, and the fever of the world,
Have hung upon the beatings of my heart--
How oft, in spirit, have I turned to thee,
O sylvan Wye! thou wanderer thro' the woods,
How often has my spirit turned to thee!
And now,
    with gleams of half-extinguished thought,
With many recognitions dim and faint,
And somewhat of a sad perplexity,
The picture of the mind revives again:
While here I stand, not only with the sense
Of present pleasure, but with pleasing thoughts
That in this moment there is life and food
For future years. And so I dare to hope,

Book of L ² - Quotable Wit and Wisdom

Though changed, no doubt, from what I was when first
I came among these hills; when like a roe
I bounded o'er the mountains, by the sides
Of the deep rivers, and the lonely streams,
Wherever nature led: more like a man
Flying from something that he dreads, than one
Who sought the thing he loved. For nature then
(The coarser pleasures of my boyish days,
And their glad animal movements all gone by)
To me was all in all.--I cannot paint
What then I was. The sounding cataract
Haunted me like a passion: the tall rock,
The mountain, and the deep and gloomy wood,
Their colours and their forms, were then to me
An appetite; a feeling and a love,

Dr. Common Sense

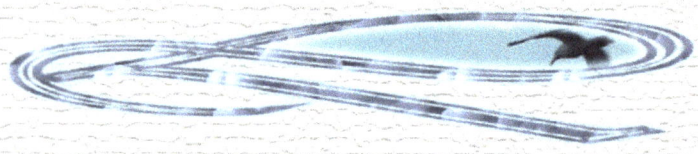

That had no need of a remoter charm,
By thought supplied, nor any interest
Unborrowed from the eye.--That time is past,
And all its aching joys are now no more,
And all its dizzy raptures. Not for this
Faint I, nor mourn nor murmur, other gifts
Have followed; for such loss, I would believe,
Abundant recompence. For I have learned
To look on nature, not as in the hour
Of thoughtless youth; but hearing oftentimes
The still, sad music of humanity,
Nor harsh nor grating, though of ample power
To chasten and subdue. And I have felt
A presence that disturbs me with the joy
Of elevated thoughts; a sense sublime
Of something far more deeply interfused,

Book of L² - Quotable Wit and Wisdom

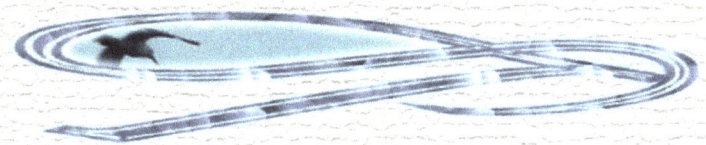

Whose dwelling is the light of setting suns,
And the round ocean and the living air,
And the blue sky, and in the mind of man;
A motion and a spirit, that impels
All thinking things, all objects of all thought,
And rolls through all things.
    Therefore am I still
A lover of the meadows and the woods,
And mountains; and of all that we behold
From this green earth; of all the mighty world
Of eye, and ear,--both what they half create,
And what perceive; well pleased to recognise
In nature and the language of the sense,
The anchor of my purest thoughts, the nurse,
The guide, the guardian of my heart, and soul
Of all my moral being.

Dr. Common Sense

Nor perchance,
If I were not thus taught, should I the more
Suffer my genial spirits to decay:
For thou art with me here upon the banks
Of this fair river; thou my dearest Friend,
My dear, dear Friend; and in thy voice I catch
The language of my former heart, and read
My former pleasures in the shooting lights
Of thy wild eyes. Oh! yet a little while
May I behold in thee what I was once,
My dear, dear Sister! and this prayer I make,
Knowing that Nature never did betray
The heart that loved her; 'tis her privilege,

Book of L² - Quotable Wit and Wisdom

Through all the years of this our life, to lead
From joy to joy: for she can so inform
The mind that is within us, so impress
With quietness and beauty, and so feed
With lofty thoughts, that neither evil tongues,
Rash judgments, nor the sneers of selfish men,
Nor greetings where no kindness is, nor all
The dreary intercourse of daily life,
Shall e'er prevail against us, or disturb
Our cheerful faith, that all which we behold
Is full of blessings. Therefore let the moon
Shine on thee in thy solitary walk;
And let the misty mountain-winds be free
To blow against thee: and, in after years,

Dr. Common Sense

When these wild ecstasies shall be matured
Into a sober pleasure; when thy mind
Shall be a mansion for all lovely forms,
Thy memory be as a dwelling-place
For all sweet sounds and harmonies; oh! then,
If solitude, or fear, or pain, or grief,
Should be thy portion,
    with what healing thoughts
Of tender joy wilt thou remember me,
And these my exhortations! Nor, perchance--
If I should be where I no more can hear
Thy voice,
    nor catch from thy wild eyes these gleams
Of past existence--wilt thou then forget
That on the banks of this delightful stream

Book of L² - Quotable Wit and Wisdom

We stood together; and that I, so long
A worshipper of Nature, hither came
Unwearied in that service: rather say
With warmer love--oh! with far deeper zeal
Of holier love. Nor wilt thou then forget,
That after many wanderings, many years
Of absence, these steep woods and lofty cliffs,
And this green pastoral landscape, were to me
More dear,
    both for themselves and for thy sake!

Dr. Common Sense

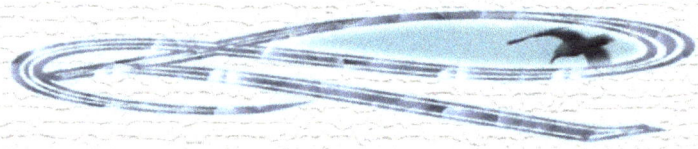

When wit and genius meet their doom,
They tell us of the fate of Rome,
The lawless herd, with fury blind,
The flowers are gone, - but still we find...

On the Same -
(On the Burning of
Lord Mansfield's Library)
William Cowper

When wit and genius meet their doom
In all devouring flame,
They tell us of the fate of Rome,
And bid us fear the same.

O'er Murray's loss the Muses wept,
They felt the rude alarm,
Yet blessed the guardian care that kept
His sacred head from harm.

Book of L [2] - Quotable Wit and Wisdom

There memory, like the bee that's fed
From Flora's balmy store,
The quintessence of all he read
Had treasured up before.

The lawless herd, with fury blind,
Have done him cruel wrong;
The flowers are gone, – but still we find
The honey on his tongue.

Dr. Common Sense

on a luminous pale-gray sky;
a long thin cloud above the colour of August rye.
Where the thin wind stung my cheeks,
and the hard snow ran in little ripples and peaks

Winter-Solitude
Archibald Lampman

I saw the city's towers
   on a luminous pale-gray sky;
Beyond them a hill of the softest mistiest green,
With naught but frost
   and the coming of night between,
And a long thin cloud above
   the colour of August rye.

Book of L² - Quotable Wit and Wisdom

I sat in the midst of a plain
>on my snowshoes with bended knee
Where the thin wind stung my cheeks,
And the hard snow
>ran in little ripples and peaks,
Like the fretted floor
>of a white and petrified sea.
And a strange peace
>gathered about my soul and shone,
As I sat reflecting there,
In a world so mystically fair,
So deathly silent---I so utterly alone.

Dr. Common Sense

A tree's leaves may be ever so good,
So may its bar, so may its wood;
Late in life I have come on fern.
Now lichens are due to have their turn

Leaves Compared with Flowers
Robert Frost

A tree's leaves may be ever so good,

So may its bar, so may its wood;
But unless you put the right thing to its root
It never will show much flower or fruit.

But I may be one who does not care
Ever to have tree bloom or bear.
Leaves for smooth and bark for rough,
Leaves and bark may be tree enough.

Book of L² - Quotable Wit and Wisdom

Some giant trees have bloom so small
They might as well have none at all.
Late in life I have come on fern.
Now lichens are due to have their turn.

I bade men tell me which in brief,
Which is fairer, flower or leaf.
They did not have the wit to say,
Leaves by night and flowers by day.

Leaves and bar, leaves and bark,
To lean against and hear in the dark.
Petals I may have once pursued.
Leaves are all my darker mood.

Dr. Common Sense

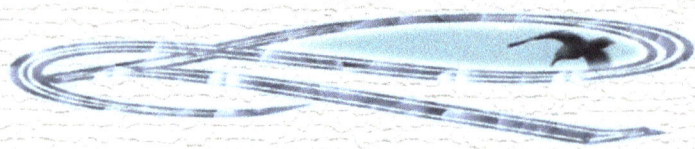

When the green woods laugh with the voice of joy,
And the dimpling stream runs laughing by;
when the meadows laugh with lively green,
And the grasshopper laughs in the merry scene

Laughing Song
William Blake

When the green woods laugh

   with the voice of joy,
And the dimpling stream runs laughing by;
When the air does laugh with our merry wit,
And the green hill laughs with the noise of it;

when the meadows laugh with lively green,
And the grasshopper laughs in the merry scene,
When Mary and Susan and Emily
With their sweet round mouths sing 'Ha, ha he!'

Book of L² - Quotable Wit and Wisdom

When the painted birds laugh in the shade,
Where our table with cherries and nuts
    is spread:
Come live, and be merry, and join with me,
To sing the sweet chorus of 'Ha, ha, he!'

Dr. Common Sense

Leman! Thy banks were lovely as to all,
But they have made them lovelier, for the lore
Of mighty minds doth hallow in the core

Sonnet to Lake Leman
Lord Byron

Rousseau -- Voltaire --

    our Gibbon -- De Staël --
Leman! these names are worthy of thy shore,
Thy shore of names like these!
    wert thou no more,
Their memory thy remembrance would recall:
To them thy banks were lovely as to all,
But they have made them lovelier, for the lore
Of mighty minds doth hallow in the core
Of human hearts the ruin of a wall

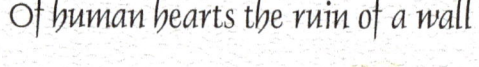

Book of L² - Quotable Wit and Wisdom

Where dwelt the wise and wondrous;
   but by thee
How much more, Lake of Beauty! do we feel,
In sweetly gliding o'er thy crystal sea,
The wild glow of that not ungentle zeal,
Which of the heirs of immortality
Is proud, and makes the breath of glory real!

Dr. Common Sense

    I leave with thee a sense
  Of hands upheld and trials rendered less,
That love, which fails of perfect utterance here,
   Lives on to fill the heavenly atmosphere

A Legacy
John Greenleaf Whittier

Friend of my many years!
When the great silence falls, at last, on me,
Let me not leave, to pain and sadden thee,
A memory of tears,
But pleasant thoughts alone.
Of one who was thy friendship's honored guest
And drank the wine of consolation pressed
From sorrows of thy own.

Book of L ^{2} - Quotable Wit and Wisdom

𝓘 leave with thee a sense
Of hands upheld and trials rendered less,
The unselfish joy which is to helpfulness
Its own great recompense.
The knowledge that from thine,
As from the garments of the Master, stole
Calmness and strength,
    the virtue which makes whole
And heals without a sign.
Yea more, the assurance strong
That love, which fails of perfect utterance here,
Lives on to fill the heavenly atmosphere
With its immortal song.

Dr. Common Sense

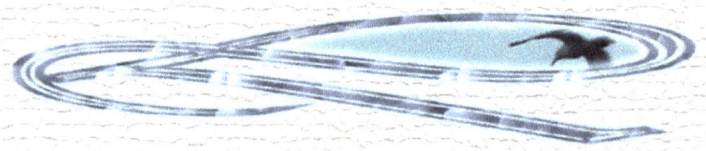

Therefore I lie with her, and she with me,
And in our faults by lies we flattered be

Sonnet 138
William Shakespeare

When my love swears
  that she is made of truth
I do believe her, though I know she lies,
That she might think me some untutored youth,
Unlearnèd in the world's false subtleties.
Thus vainly thinking that she thinks me young,
Although she knows my days are past the best,
Simply I credit her false-speaking tongue;
On both sides thus is simple truth suppressed.

Book of L ² - Quotable Wit and Wisdom

But wherefore says she not she is unjust?
And wherefore say not I that I am old?
O, love's best habit is in seeming trust,
And age in love, loves not to have years told.
Therefore I lie with her, and she with me,
And in our faults by lies we flattered be.
.

Publisher's Blog:
WcP Blog | World Culture Pictorial
www.worldculturepictorial.com

"This is awesome!
Your photos are perfectly taken!
It captured the decisive moment.
I am a fan already."
- Sarah

"Thanks for trying to
make the world a better place."
- Anonymous

"Amazing site,
worth the visit every time...
enjoy."
- Sam

Dr. Common Sense

Other Books of L

hardcover and paperback:
www.worldculturepictorial.com/book-of-L.html

Book of L ^{2} - Quotable Wit and Wisdom

Other Books of L

coming soon:
www.worldculturepictorial.com/book-of-L.html

www.ingramcontent.com/pod-product-compliance
Lightning Source LLC
Chambersburg PA
CBHW042044280426
43661CB00094B/1002